TAKE NO MORE NOTICE

Gordon Irving has written many books including *Great Scot!*, the biography of Harry Lauder, *The Wit of the Scots*, *The Wit of Robert Burns*, and *Brush Up Your Scotland*. Together with illustrator Ian Heath he is responsible for the highly successful *Take No Notice*. He is an internationally famous showbusiness journalist, and a world authority on ludicrous signs and notices.

Ian Heath is a talented young cartoonist whose drawings have appeared in *Punch*, the *Daily Mirror*, the *Sun*, *Mayfair*, *Penthouse* and many other publications both in Britain and the USA. As well as illustrating the *Take No Notice* series, his drawings have accompanied *The Two Ronnies: And It's Hello From Him*, *Time For A Few Extra Items* and *And It's Goodbye From Him*. He has also compiled and illustrated his own selection of gems from Lonely Hearts columns entitled *Stupid Cupid*.

TAKE NO MORE NOTICE

Compiled by
Gordon Irving
Illustrated by
Ian Heath

Star

A STAR BOOK
published by
the Paperback Division of
W.H. ALLEN & Co Ltd

A Star Book
Published in 1982
by the Paperback Division of
W.H. Allen & Co. Ltd
A Howard and Wyndham Company
44 Hill Street, London W1X 8LB

Copyright © Gordon Irving and Ian Heath 1982

Phototypeset by Tradespools Limited, Frome, Somerset
Printed and bound in Great Britain by
Cox & Wyman Ltd, Reading

ISBN 0352 311940

To Whom It May Concern ...

This collection of hundreds more of the world's funniest signs and notices is dedicated to the thousands of readers across the globe who are happily making a fun hobby out of collecting more odd and rib-tickling signs and notices for the next in our Take No Notice series.

Collectors, professional as well as amateur, should send their latest gems to Gordon Irving c/o Star Books, 44 Hill Street, London W1X 8LB.

In a wool shop in Durham:

Don't believe those who say we don't give a darn

Notice in an estate-agent's window in Croydon:
Bargain, well-maintained Victorian house, with guaranteed
dry rot throughout.

In a slimming clinic in Kensington:
Here today, gaunt tomorrow.

On a wayside pulpit in the English Midlands:
Work for the Lord – the Fringe
Benefits are Out of This World.

In an evening newspaper in York:
For sale, Toilet-seat cover. Barely used.

In a surgical-wear shop in Toronto:
Trust us to truss you.

In an Aberdeen restaurant:
In case of fire, don't panic. First pay the bill, then run like hell.

Sign near a cemetery in San Jose, California:
Second-hand tombstone for sale.
Extraordinary bargain for family named Schwarzendorfer.

In a lawyer's office in Indianapolis:
One way to stop people from jumping down your throat is
to keep your mouth shut.

In a pub in Devon:
If you really need glasses, please don't take ours. Go to an
optician.

In a talent agent's office in New York:
Keep on trying. It's better to be a has-been than a never-
will-be.

Notice outside a demolished cinema in Liverpool:
Gone With The Wind.

Notice in a newsagent's window in Oban, Scotland:
Lost, ginger cat called Chips. Answers to Fish.

In a bakery window in Vancouver:
Closed for two weeks.
We Kneaded the Break.

In a reducing clinic in Winnipeg, Canada:
Overweight? It could be just your desserts.

Sign above a closed-down shop in Hull:
See! We DID undersell everyone.

Outside a church in Dublin:
Genesis is Good for You.

In a tyre depot in Glasgow:
We Skid You Not.

Sign at a demolition site in Detroit:
Wanted, capable man to handle dynamite. Must be
prepared to travel long distances.

In a jeweller's in Piccadilly, London:
Let Us Give You a Gilt Complex.

In a moneylender's office:
Before borrowing money from a friend, decide which you
need more – the money or your friend.

In china section of a Birmingham department store:
Touch if you must,
Pay up if you bust.

Outside a nudist camp in California:
If you happen to see us while driving by, it's not necessary to wave.

Sign in an accountant's office in Giffnock, Glasgow:
Inflation is what happens when you are broke with a lot of money in your pocket.

On a hospital notice-board in Manchester:
Dangerous drugs must be locked up with the ward sister.

Notice in a fish-and-chip shop in Dumbarton, Scotland:
We Fry Harder.

In an estate-agent's window in Christchurch, New Zealand:
Owing to our firm policy of expansion involving several new offices, these premises will be closing.

Sign outside the lavatory door in the path lab of a New York hospital:
Staph only.

In a ladies' beautifying salon in Melbourne:
Our treatment covers a multitude of chins.

In a garage forecourt in Kent:
A driver is safer when the road is dry;
The road is safer when the driver is dry.

Advert in a Bristol newspaper:
To let, flat with three rooms, kitchen, bathroom, plus outside toilet at present occupied by owner.

In a used-car saleroom in Devon:
We always drive a good bargain.

Notice on thermostat of a hotel in Kobe, Japan:
You do not have to get yourself hot in this room. Please control yourself.

In a cosmetic-surgeon's waiting-room:
Sometimes the Eyes have it –
More often it's the Nose.

Notice in fish'n'chip café in south London:
Batter late than never.

In perfumery department of a London store:
We can supply the Know-How But Not The Common Scents.

In a jeweller's window in Edmonton, Canada:
We stock counterfeit jewels . . .
They won't TELL unless you do!

On notice-board in a Cardiff social club:
The trouble with telling a good story is that it nearly always reminds the other fellow of a bad one.

Sign at a car repair yard in Dover:
Leave your body in our hands.

In a second-hand bookshop in London's Soho:
The covers of our books may be a little bit dirty . . . but the stories aren't.

In window of a shop in a recession-hit town:
Buy now – while shop lasts.

On a university notice-board:
"The End of the World." Lunch afterwards.

Notice in a moneylender's office in Glasgow:
Stay Friends with Us . . . Until Debt Us Do Part!

Outside a stock-car racing track:
We offer Bangers and Smash

Outside a store in Edinburgh selling Scottish kilts:
Buy here and you'll never say you couldn't do a fling with it.

In a restaurant for slimming fanatics:
Our dishes will take your breadth away.

In a home with five teenagers:
Make someone happy – get off the phone!

Sign above door of a village store:
Mind your head – Falling Prices

Notice in a shop window in Manchester:
Lost, mongrel dog with bad limp due to road accident; ear badly scarred in fight; wall-eyed; slightly deaf; answers to the name 'Lucky'.

In a tax-adviser's office:
The tax inspector has got what it takes to take what you've got.

In the swimwear section of a store in Southampton:
Our bikinis are like your garden gate . . . they guard the property without obscuring the view.

In a driving-school in the English Midlands:
Crash Courses: Available For Those Who Wish to Learn to Drive QUICKLY.

Sign outside a New York church:
Life is Fragile – Handle it with Prayer.

Notice above a display of new brassieres in a Leeds store:
Ladies, This is the Real Decoy.

On the breakfast menu of a hotel at Auchtermuchty, Scotland:
Porridge – Our Oat Cuisine.

In a driving-school in Oxford:
It's always the OVERtakers who keep the UNDERtakers busy.

In a jeweller's window in Birmingham:
Give the little lady something to wrap around her finger apart from yourself.

In a shoe shop:
We doctor and heel your shoes, save your soles, and see to your dyeing.

Billboard outside a Manchester theatre after a performance of 'Jesus Christ Superstar':
You've seen the show . . . now read the book.

Nameplate notice in Sligo, Eire:
Argue & Phibbs, Solicitors.

Notice on board in a men-only club:
Woman is one of nature's agreeable blunders.

Notice in window of an old-worldly cottage in Cornwall:
No parking, please. This window has been in constant use
for over 200 years.

On a tycoon's notice-board in downtown New York:
One of the great advantages of success is that you don't have
to listen to good advice any more!

In a marriage-guidance office in Piccadilly London:
Love is going home and putting your feet up before a
roaring wife.

Sign in a town in Surrey:
RED ARROWS FLYING DISPLAY TODAY.
Below, someone has scrawled:
If wet, in Town Hall.

Sign in window of a fruit shop in Edinburgh:
Vampires please note – Blood Oranges now available.

Notice in window of a London café:
Why don't you eat here, and keep the wife as a pet?

In a photographic shop:
Dark room for lovers. Quick developments.

On a billboard in East Anglia:
Theatre Royal, Norwich
Coach trips from Beccles and Bungay to . . .
    Jesus Christ Wed. 18th
    Des O'Connor Wed. 25th

Sign at a petrol station in the North of England:
Drive Carefully – The Kids Expect You Home.

In a beauty salon in Manchester:
Come in here and stop your husband reading between the lines.

Notice in a New York pet store:
Buy a bird-cage today – use yesterday's nest-egg.

In a shop in Edinburgh:
Try our easy terms. 100 per cent down and nothing more to pay.

In an office in Toronto:
Business is like a black eye. You have to fight to get it.

Sign in a London shoe shop:
We foot everything but the bill.

Notice above door of the Ladies' Room in a Glasgow night-club:
This rest room is for the use of ladies only. In case of emergency, use fire escape.

In the window of a store in Auckland, New Zealand:
Don't get overcharged in other shops – come in here!

In window of a restaurant in Blackpool:
Wanted – man to wash dishes and two waitresses.

Outside an antique shop in Oxford, England:
Modern antiques our speciality.

On a church notice-board in Yorkshire:
People who tell you what kind of people they are, usually aren't!

Sign in window of a shoe-repairer's:
Nothing CORNY in our work. Everything done by SOLE proprietor.

Scrawled over a major dent in a Mini:
Hit someone your own size!

In a shoe shop:
It is no feet for us to fit fat feet.

Notice outside a haunted house in Ye Olde England:
We offer ghost-to-ghost tours.

In a butcher's shop in Bristol:
We will give you nothing to beef about.

In a pawn shop in Birmingham:
For you a-loan.

Notice in lawyer's office in Malta:
One way to stop people from jumping down your throat is
to keep your mouth shut.

On a church billboard in Boston, USA:
If you are sitting on top of the world, remember, it turns
over every twenty-four hours.

In a London job shop:
A baby-sitter is a teenager who comes in to act like an adult
while the adults go out and act like teenagers!

Sign in an olde English churchyard:
As maintenance costs are rising every month, parishioners
are asked to kindly cut the grass around their own graves.

Sign outside a store selling curtains:
Come right in now and HANG the consequences!

Notice in a Pakistani restaurant:
Eat here – Allah carte.

In a gift shop in Chicago:
For the man who has everything – a calendar to remind him when his payments are due.

Sign at a caravan exhibition:
Have a home while looking for a place to park.

In a lavatory in a London pub:
My mother made me a homosexual.
Scrawled underneath:
If I get her the wool, would she make me one, too?

In a window of a house in New York:
Piano lessons. Special pains given to beginners.

Advertisement in a weekly newspaper in Essex:
For sale. Four-birth caravan.

Notice in a railroad engineer's office in Kansas: ✓
When two trains are approaching each other at a crossing,
they shall both come to a full stop, and neither shall start up
until the other has gone.

Sign on a butcher's scale in Luton:
The weigh of all flesh.

Notice in window of a Liverpool café:
Self Service. No waiting.

Sign outside a school in Brisbane:
Drivers, take care – do not kill a child.   ✓
Below, a child has written:
Wait for a teacher.

In a health-food store in Chicago:
Our diets are for people who are thick and tired of dieting.

In a beauty salon in Los Angeles:
We Give the Breast Results.

In a Dublin money-lender's office:
Money talks – sometimes it screams!

Sign in a job-centre in London:
Watch-repairer required to start this minute. Must be a good timekeeper.

On door of a house in Middlesex:
Postman, kindly latch our front gate behind you. (Signed) The Dog.
Chalked below:
'Stop chewing my pants first! (Signed) The Postman.'

In a psychiatrist's office in New York:
Anyone who comes to a psychiatrist needs his head examined!

In a dentist's surgery in Milngavie, near Glasgow:
Now that this little session is over
May we say to you:
'Fang you very much!'

Printed at the foot of a menu in Toronto:
"This may be a take-away joint, but that doesn't mean customers can take away our menu cards."

Sticker on rear window of a car in Durban, South Africa:
I'm not a dirty old lady. I'm a sexy senior citizen.

Notice in a slimming clinic in Eastbourne:
Make sure you only TIP our scales. Don't BRIBE them.

On the notice-board in a London banking house:
It is better to be stupid like everyone than to be clever like no one.

Notice on a doorstep in Croydon:
No Milk Today. By Today I Mean Tomorrow As I Wrote
This Yesterday.

In reception suite of a New York marriage-guidance bureau:
Remember, the honeymoon is over when HE says he'll be late for dinner, and SHE's already left a note saying it's in the fridge.

Sign in a city board-room:
The bigger a man's head grows, the easier it is to fill his shoes.

On notice-board in a ladies' only social club:
Gossip is when you hear something you like about somebody you know.

In a garage forecourt in Coventry:
All puncture repairs done at flat rate.

Notice on a tomato stall in the West Country:
The management reserves the right to pinch back.

Notice in a laundry near Belfast:
Don't kill the wife, let us do the dirty work.

In window of a restaurant in Great Yarmouth:
Tired and thin, totter in. Strong and stout, swagger out.

Advertisement in the New York subway:
Mike's Funeral Parlor. Ten per cent discount on all services during the month of August.

On a notice-board at Glasgow University: ✓
Think before you speak – and you will find yourself with a lot less to talk about!

In a dentist's surgery in Cairo:
I extract other people's teeth to find employment for my own.

At an inn in the English Lake District:
Three-coarse lunches – £1-15

Notice in a confectioner's store in Blackpool:
Delicious Blackpool rock – take your pick.

In a psychiatrist's waiting-room:
It is so silly to lose your temper, nobody wants to find it.

In a doctor's reception room:
Keep Smiling! It Makes People Wonder What You Are Up To.

In the bedding section of a department store:
Come In and Drowse Around.

Sign outside a nudist colony:
Sorry, Clothed for Winter.

Notice on windscreen of a car parked in centre of Glasgow:
I think traffic wardens are nice people. PS: Back in ten minutes!

Outside a social club in Dundee:
Closed Tonight for Official Opening.

On an office notice-board in Swansea:
When easy does it, somebody usually has to do it again.

In a health-and-fitness shop in Windsor:
Middle age is when you start eating what is good for you
instead of what you like.

In a men's outfitters:
Our trews are stronger than fiction.

On a company president's desk in Chicago:
If you work faithfully 8 hours a day, you may eventually get
to be a boss and work 12 hours a day.

Notice in a boarding-house in South London:
Young men taken in and done for.

On a school wall in Dumbarton, Scotland:
Down with teachers . . .
Below, a pupil has chalked:
. . . knickers!

In rear window of car in Liverpool:
Caution! Unexpected Stops. Wife Learning to Drive.

In a village store selling knitting material:
We Won't Pull the Wool Over Anybody's Eyes.

In a second-hand furniture shop in Carlisle:
For Sale, Smoker's Chair. Solid Ash.

Notice in a bus station in Dublin:
Our service is normal on Sunday – except for certain
cancellations, alterations and additions.

On a church notice-board in Winnipeg, Canada:
Bring yourself to worship, not your clothes!

Notice in office of a psychiatrist:
Tact is that rare talent for not admitting you were right in the first place.

In window of village store on a sleepy Scottish Hebridean island:
Yesterday's papers tomorrow, 3pm

Notice on a public hoarding in Southern Ireland:
Illiterate? WRITE Today for Free Help.

Sign in a window of a pet-bird store in Dallas, Texas:
All Is Not Sold That Twitters.

Piece of graffiti spotted on a London wall:
Schizophrenia divides and rules, OK?

Notice in a Glasgow optician's:
We Can Make You See Eye to Eye.

Outside a dry-cleaner's in Fuengirola, Southern Spain:
Drop Your Trousers Here For Best Results.

Sign in an osteopath's:
We Rub You Up The Right Way.

In an estate-agent's office in Birmingham, England:
Here is an opportunity to purchase a charming house at a
price which bears no relation to its cost.

Note in a bottle outside a house in North London:
One loaf and one sliced milk.

Notice in a divorce-lawyer's office:
A pity about Eve! She couldn't tell Adam what a wonderful
man her first husband was.

Epitaph in Ripon Cathedral churchyard, England:
Here lies poor but honest Bryan Tinstall. He was a most
expert angler until Death, envious of his merit, threw out
his line, hooked him and landed him here the 21st day of
April 1790.

Notice in a marriage-guidance bureau:
A man needs a wife because, sooner or later, something is bound to happen that he can't blame on the Government.

Notice in a bank in Philadelphia, USA:
The easiest thing to get on credit is a reputation for not paying your bill.

Notice outside an open-air cinema in an Indian village:
Patrons viewing the film from outside the boundary walls are requested not to sit on the back of camels or in branches of trees.

Sign over a wine display in a Brighton wine-and-spirits store:
For connoisseurs. The Beaune that's worth working your fingers to.

Sign outside a New York church:
CHCH is no good unless UR in it.

On rear window of a well-worn British car in France:
Brest or Bust.

Notice in a flower shop in Melbourne:
Come In – Just For The Smell of It.

On notice-board of a girls' school:
Following the sex-instruction class, all girls will assemble for lessons in judo and self-defence.

Sign in a North Wales café:
In a hurry? Why not have coffee and roll downstairs?

Sign in a marriage bureau in Wellington, New Zealand:
It is impossible to please the whole world and your mother-in-law as well.

In window of a butcher's shop in Fort William, Scotland: √
Credit given only to people over 75 accompanied by their parents.

Notice outside booking office of railway station at Clydebank, Scotland:
Open 11 a.m. for sale of season tickets. No trains running.

Outside a country hotel famous for its ghost:
Dread and Breakfast. Be our guest.

Sign in a bookshop in Detroit:
Curdle up with a good murder mystery.

Notice in a pub in Bolton:
Why risk a hangover? Stay drunk!

Notice in a busy restaurant at Scarborough:
Eat, drink and be merry, for tomorrow you may diet!

Outside a dairy near Bristol:
You can't beat our milk, but you can whip our cream.

Notice in a car-repairer's:
Women are creatures who wrap men either around their little fingers or around their front bumpers.

Notice in honeymoon suite of a San Francisco hotel:
Love is being willing to share your toothbrush with someone else.

On a managing director's desk in London's Regent Street:
Never forget – a mistake is evidence that someone has tried to do something.

On a company president's desk in Los Angeles:
There is no failure except in no longer trying.

Notice on a large cardboard box on a market stall in Preston, England:
'Slightly Soiled'
The contents – ladies' knickers.

Sign in an old folks' club in Philadelphia, USA:
The nicest thing about growing older is that it takes such a long time.

In a jeweller's window in Hollywood:
Eternity rings. Twelve months guarantee.

Printer's error on tickets for a 'Naughty Nineties' dance near Birmingham, England:
Enjoy Yourself for £2-50. Naughty Nighties Night.

On a church notice-board in New York:
If you think the going is too easy, take another look. You may well be going downhill.

In a café in Great Yarmouth:
The prices we quote are for meals only. Cutlery extra if you wish to take away!

In window of a hair salon in Winnipeg, Canada:
Let us tame your wild March hair.

In a florist's in Southport, England:
Roses are red,
Violets are blue,
Gone to lunch –
We blossom at two.

In a pub in rural Devon:
Drinkers who leave while the room is in motion will be
doing so at their own risk.

On the rear of a furniture removal truck:
You will be carried away by our moving performance.

In window of a confectioner's in Blackpool:
Try our chocolate-coconut-creams – and furnish your
mouth with the cheapest three-piece sweet in town.

Notice in a restaurant in Birmingham:
We Collect Taxes – Income T. and Value Added. In Between Times We Also Serve Value Added Food.

In a joke-shop in New York:
Our prices won't make you die laughing but our jokes will.

Notice in a bank in London:
Inflation today simply means being flat broke with a lot of money in your pocket.

Outside a garden centre in Aberdeen Scotland:
Best-quality top soil here – dirt cheap.

Sign above a dictionary in a London book shop:
Say it with Fowler's.

Notice in a foreign embassy in Paris:
An international crisis is like sex – as long as you keep talking about it, nothing happens.

In a job shop in Birmingham:
When you are down and out, something always turns up –
and it's usually the noses of your friends.

Notice in an estate-agent's window in England's Shakespeare country:
Fine Old Period Property . . . Now Nearing Completion.

Notice in theatre foyer in Los Angeles:
Definitely The Show of the Year. All Tickets Will Be Sold
on a First-come First-served basis.

Sign in a Civil Service office corridor:
Tea Trolleys Have Right of Way.

Notice in a New Orleans bookshop:
We earn our living by the sweat of your browse.

In classified columns of The Times:
Jimmy Edwards has not sent Christmas cards this year,
owing to Christmas having arrived sooner than expected.

On a wayside pulpit in New Orleans, USA:
Sour grapes have upset a lot of apple carts.

*Note on windscreen of car illegally parked on an Edinburgh
street:*
Been round the square 10 times, can't find parking place.
Forgive us our trespasses. – Reverend J. Mitchell
*Two hours later the Reverend Mitchell returned to find this note
alongside a parking ticket:*
Been round the square 10 years. If I don't book you, I lose
my job. Lead us not into temptation. – Traffic warden.

*Notice beside an expensive-looking red box in a London gift-
shop:*
For the woman who wants to go all the way . . .!
Inside the box – a road map of Great Britain.

Sign in a sewing-machine shop in Sydney, Australia:
There's No Bizness like Sewbiz.

Notice in a photographer's studio:
Some day my prints will come.

In an electrical store window in Toronto:
Shock it to us!

Notice in a fire station in Coventry:
Even our married firemen have lots of old flames.

In a nursery selling potted plants: ✓
Be tactful. Please do not talk to our plants unless you are going to buy them.

On rear window of a car in Philadelphia, USA:
The Majority is Not Silent. The Government is Deaf.

Sign in a barber's shop in Sheffield:
If not completely satisfied, your hair refunded.

On notice-board of a commercial office in Johannesburg:
Brains are never a handicap to a woman if she's smart
enough to hide them under a see-through blouse.

*On a tree in a London park someone has carved a heart with this
message:*
Henry Loves Susannah.
Underneath, someone has chiselled out a second message:
This report is unconfirmed.

Notice in a newsagent's window:
Will the person or persons who borrowed my lawn-mower
please return it as I have another chance to lend it out.

On a bulletin board of a Government office:
Things Are Going from Bad to Worse – Retroactively.

In a psychologist's reception-office:
The art of communicating with a woman is to hear what she
doesn't say.

Placard carried by hitchhiker on an American freeway:
Undecided Voter. Pick Me Up and Convince Me.

Notice at the complaints desk of a department store:
We'd Like to Help You Out. Which Way Did You Come In?

Sign on a roadside in Hawaii:
Children Playing. Please Drive Tenderly.

Sticker on a fast sports car driven by a pretty blonde:
Honk if you don't want to sleep alone tonight!

On a tree in the middle of the road near Seville, Spain:
This Tree Hits Cars Only in Self-Defence.

On a railway crossing in the Scottish Highlands:
He Looked, She Didn't . . . He IS, She Isn't!

On the desk of a company president in Fifth Avenue, New York:
Don't Start Telling Me What I Mean – Let Me Figure It Out Myself.

In a divorce lawyer's office:
The man who thinks he's smarter than his wife is married to a clever woman.

Notice in a beauty salon in Cheltenham:
Poise means lifting your eyebrows instead of the roof!

Sign in a department store in Montreal:
Towels for the whole damp family.

Notice beside a bowl of peanuts in a Californian bar:
The Drinking Man's Filter.

On a newly-seeded lawn in Brighton:
Dog Keep Off. Owner is Vicious.

Notice in the office of a High Court judge:
I Agree With Everything You Are Saying But I Must Admit You Are Wrong.

Sign in jeweller's window in Stockholm:
Watches repaired. Cuckoo clocks psycho-analysed.

Notice in a cinema in New York:
Our usherettes are paid to put you in your place.

Notice in a marriage-counselling office in Stockholm:
A successful marriage requires falling in love many times,
but always with the same person.

In a slimming clinic in Miami:
Beware of the Noah Problem – don't take two of everything.

Notice in a driving-school in Glasgow:
Driving with one hand on the wheel and one hand on the
girl satisfies neither the Highway Patrol nor the girl.

Chalked on a sidewalk in San Francisco:
John Feels An Inordinate Degree of Ambivalence Towards
Mary.

Sign in an Italian restaurant in London:
If you don't like Italian food, you're anti-pasta.

Sign in an office in Fifth Avenue, New York:
Don't Be Indispensable. If You Can't Be Replaced, You
Can't Be Promoted.

Notice in a Happy-Marriages Bureau in Honolulu:
Marry in Haste, Repeat at Leisure.

In a newsagent's shop window in Bedford:
Good home wanted for Staffordshire bull terrier. Almost human, but otherwise sound.

On a notice board at Cambridge University:
An Intellectual is a man who takes more words than necessary to tell more than he knows.

Notice in a dog-kennels in Dallas, Texas:
Money will buy you a pretty good dog but it won't buy the wag of his tail.

In a partner-dating office in New York:
Never let a fool kiss you or a kiss fool you.

On notice-board of a driving-school in Manchester:
Why Not Give Yourself an 'L' of a Chance?

In a dentist's waiting-room in Christchurch, New Zealand:
We Won't Pull A Fast One On You.

Sign in a Belfast slimming clinic:
Tubby or not tubby, fat is the question!

Card in a shop window in Cardiff:
For sale – handsome Basset Hound. Can be seen at above address in the evening – or heard within a two-mile radius at dawn.

Notice in hospital clinic:
Blood donors wanted. Help keep us in the RED.

On a stocking counter in a city department store:
Your Face May Be Your FORTUNE, but it's your legs that draw INTEREST.

In a tax consultant's office in London:
Look after the pence, and the tax-man will take care of the pounds.

On a church notice-board in Leeds:
Our home-made claret competition was a big success.
Winners – Mrs Arnold (fruity, well-rounded), Mrs
Stephens (fine colour and full-bodied) and Miss Smith
(slightly acid).

71

Notice on windscreen of a car in a supermarket park at Prestwick, Scotland:
Don't block this car. My wife's in her ninth month.

In a paint shop in Los Angeles:
Husbands ordering specially mixed colours must have signed note from their wives.

In a dress shop in New York:
We Have Guise for Dolls.

Sign in a maternity hospital in Melbourne:
Call Us Any Time, Night or Day. We Always DELIVER.

Outside a Methodist Church in Gloucester:
Come In Now For A Faith Lift.

On a demand note from a firm in Glasgow:
Please note – this invoice is now so overdue the original was written on papyrus!

Above a large bowl of English pennies on a market stall in Coventry:
Pennies – Two Pence Each.

On notice-board in a trade union office in London:
A Dangerous Fanatic is someone who would be a Dedicated Idealist if he happened to be on your side.

Sign in a hardware store in San Francisco:
If it weren't for Venetian blinds, it would be curtains for us.

Notice on office wall in Glasgow:
If you keep blowing your own horn, people are going to be quick to get out of your way.

On a badly smashed-up car on a Welsh hillside:
Wow! Now Will You Belt Up!

On a tombstone in an English cemetery:
Here lies Joshua Ransom, died August 6, 1654. His widow, 24, mourns but can be comforted.

In window of a boarding-house in Llandudno:
Young Maid Servant Wanted – Able to Do the Work of a Small Horse.

Notice in a joke and magic store in Chicago:
Sale. Unbelievable Bargains Until You See 'Em!

Outside a church in Perth, Australia:
Congregation members wanted. No experience necessary.

Above toy bones in a pet-food shop in Luton:
Make sure your pooch is never bone-idle.

Sign in holiday-town selling sun-glasses:
Look through our glasses darkly.

Scrawled on wall of a college in California:
To do is to be – Socrates
To be is to do – Sartre
Oo be do be do – Sinatra

Outside a church in Cheltenham:
All New Sermons – Unlike TV, No Summertime Repeats!

Notice in a bank in San Francisco:
Don't Kiss Our Girls. They're All Tellers.

Sign in a marriage bureau in Kentucky, USA:
Kissing don't last. Cookery do!

In a money-lender's office:
A good financier is one who can borrow money on the
strength of what he owes.

Picket sign in a cemetery:
No one lowered until we are raised.

Outside a motel in Nevada, USA:
We Take Tourists.
Underneath, someone has scrawled:
"You can say that again!"

Notice in a social club for humans in Yorkshire:
Leave all brooding to hens, worrying to puppies, chattering
to magpies, and repeating things to parrots.

On the back of a long trailer on the M6 motorway:
This is my end. Don't make it yours.

Notice in kitchen of a church hall in Torquay:
Will ladies kindly empty teapots and kettles an then stand
upside down in the sink.

In a doctor's waiting room in Exeter:
When trouble and sickness we've begotten,
To God and doctor we go for help.
When troubles and sickness have departed
God and doctor's soon forgotten.

In a pub in Doncaster:
One for the Road Could Be The Pint of No Return.

In a slimming clinic:
Waist Not, Want Not!

Notice in dentist's surgery in Perth:
We Are Your Best Filling Station.

In a savings bank in New York:
Always Borrow from a Pessimist – He Doesn't Expect his
Money Back.

On a public relations manager's desk:
Tact is the ability to describe others as they see themselves.

In a marriage-guidance office in London:
A clever wife sees through her husband – a good wife sees him through.

Notice in Douglas, Isle of Man:
Buy our Lucky Pixies
These Replicas are the
Only Original Models

In a Toronto grill-room:
We Succeed in Business Without Really Frying

In shoe-shop window at Bournemouth:
Don't Stand Two Feet Away From Comfort.

In a Chicago store selling health-and-fitness gear:
This Appliance Will Reduce Your Hips – or Bust.

Notice in a Spanish hotel:
Dinner on tomorrow's trip to Madrid will be provided free since the cost has already been added to the original price of ticket.

Notice on door of a public hall in Manchester:
Lecture on Clairvoyance cancelled – owing to unforeseen circumstances.

In window of a painter and decorator's in Carlisle:
Your Ceilings Can Be Whitewashed Any Colour.

On rear of a London milk-float:
You may keep our milkman, but kindly return the empty bottles.

Sign on a beach in California:
If you with litter will disgrace,
And Spoil the Beauty of This Place,
May Indigestion Rack Your Chest,
And Ants Invade Your Pants and Vest.

On a freshly-seeded lawn in New England:
Please Keep Off. We're Expecting.

Notice in a photographer's studio:
The rarest thing in the world is a woman who is pleased with a photograph of herself.

Advert. in a Las Vegas newspaper:
Will the man who picked up mink coat at the Dunes Hotel
Sunday night please return the smart blonde who was in it.
No questions asked – Lonely husband.

Rear-window sticker on a car in Edinburgh:
Love thy neighbour. Only, don't let they neighbour's husband catch you!

Notice on a car wash in Los Angeles:
All foreign cars will be washed with Perrier water.

Road sign in Missouri:
Main Highway Open for Traffic while Detour is being Re-paved.

In window of a ladies' lingerie shop in London:
Get romantic. We have slips that passion the night.

Notice on a brand-new washing-machine:
When all else fails, try reading the directions.

Sign outside a cathedral in an English city:
Since there is no swimming-pool on the inside, it is therefore unnecessary for tourists to visit in beach wear.

Notice in a service-station forecourt off the M1 motorway:
If you really want to let the rest of the world go by, make sure you drive within the speed limit.

In a post-office in Tehran:
Try our Persian to Persian calls.

Notice in slimming-clinic close to New York's Wall Street:
For stocky brokers.

In a Chicago clockmaker's window:
Our clocks are the tock of the town.

On notice-board of a college debating hall:
An argument is where two people are trying to get the LAST word in FIRST!

Sign on a stall in a country market in Oxfordshire:
Our fruit is ripe for eating – absolutely no teeth required.

On rear of a large truck in South Wales:
Beware, sudden tea brakes.

Notice at a health farm:
A little yearning is a dangerous thing.

In a dentist's surgery:
Let us PULL a fast one on you!

Notice beside a run-down motor-car in a used-vehicle showroom:
We guarantee full hoarse power.

Notice in a Vancouver seedsman's catalogue:
Advise us if your neighbour has a flower or plant that he is specially proud of. We can supply seeds of one larger or in an entirely new colour.

Sign outside a chapel in Boston, USA:
This is the Gateway to Heaven.
Below, this notice:
Closed during months of July and August.

Notice in barber's shop in Leeds:
I need your head to run my business.

Sign on rear window of a Rolls-Royce in London's West End:
Yes, WE are the JONESes!

Notice in hotel bedroom in Malta:
If your wife is suffering from a headache, please ring for the chambermaid.

Sign in a New York slimming clinic:
Even if you're shaped like a 'cello We can make you fit as a fiddle.

Notice in a sports store in Montreal:
Tennis balls going cheap – First Come, First Serve.

Notice in a Johannesburg swimming-pool:
If you drink, don't dive.

On a company president's desk in Boston, USA:
If it weren't for the last minute, an awful lot of things would never get done.

In a reducing salon in Dallas, Texas:
Level with us. Does your end really justify the jeans?

Notice on a park lawn in Montreal:
YOUR Feet Are Killing Me.

In a real-estate office window in a London suburb:
Buy Land Now. It's Not Being Made Any More.

South of Madrid the Spanish road authorities, catering for British drivers, put up a large detour sign with an English translation:
DETOUR PLEASE – DRIVE SIDEWAYS

Notice in a restaurant in Majorca:
We Are Open Seven Days A Week, Including Sundays.

In a marriage-counselling bureau in California:
For some people marriage is like peanuts. It's hard to stop at one.

In a department store in Milan:
This door is alarmed. Do not enter.

Notice on a farm in Oregon:
No Huntin', No Fishin', No Nuthin'.

In a church magazine at Glasgow, Scotland:
Cushioned-seats are being installed for the congregation
They should be more comfortable to sin on.

On a wayside pulpit in New York State:
If you were on trial for being a Christian, would there be enough evidence to convict you?

Sign in a national park in North America:
It is forbidden to throw stones at this notice.

In a loan office in Manchester:
Everybody should live within his means these days – even if he has to borrow to do it.

On a notice-board in a Government office in Glasgow:
We must economise – no matter how much it costs.

A notice on a college bulletin board in London read:
Shoes are required to eat in the cafeteria.
Beneath, someone has scribbled:
Socks may eat wherever they want to.

Notice in a church bulletin:
The minister's sermon on Sunday will be 'How Can We Deal With the World Crisis?' Mrs Robertson will sing 'Search Me, Oh God'.

In a lawyer's office in California:
Divorces $85. Satisfaction Guaranteed or Your Partner Back!

Sign in a gymnasium in Detroit:
We close on Sundays to Let the Soul Catch Up With the Body.

Notice on a bus in New York:
Did You Make New York Dirty Today?
Underneath, someone has scribbled:
Not nearly as dirty as New York made me.

Advert in a San Francisco newspaper:
Apartment wanted large enough to keep wife from going home to mother, small enough to keep mother from coming here.

In a law court in Philadelphia:
Stretch the Truth and your Story will wear Thin.

Sign in a supermarket in Melbourne:
Compare today's low prices – with next week's!

Sign at a crematorium car-park:
Positively No Exit from Here.

In a veterinary-surgeon's reception room:
True love is when you spend £50 for an operation on a £5 dog.

Sign in a restaurant:
Special prices 5 to 7 pm. Remember, the early bird catches the worm.

Notice in a shoe shop window:
We foot everything but the bill.

In a hospital ward in Manchester:
Male patients are warned – Do not take a turn for the NURSE.

Sign in a London betting-shop:
I am the Wizard of Odds.

At a bus station in Liverpool:
There will be no last bus from here tonight.

Outside a motor-cycle shop:
Ladies, it's warmer in our combinations.

Notice on door of a music shop in Vancouver:
Gone for lunch. Bach at two, Offenbach sooner.

In a psychiatrist's office in London:
Doctor is on holiday. In emergency, write to Evelyn Home.

In a service station on Britain's M6 motorway:
If petrol attendant is not here, ring the bell, blow horn. If
that doesn't work, – just YELL Good and Loud.

sing in a backstreet shop selling video-cassettes:
Enjoy Our Special MOvies In the PIRACY of Your Home.

On a church notice-board in Luton:
the try-angle will take you round the hardest of corners.

In an ironmonger's in Glasgow:
A handle to your name will open many doors.

In a psychiatrist's surgery:
Tact is that rare talent for not quite telling the truth.

Notice outside a boutique in England's West Country:
We can't find a cute enough name. Just call us The Shop
That Sells Expensive Imported Things and Is Run By A
Rich Widow To Keep Herself Busy.

In a cinema foyer in Toronto:
There's nothing like the new TV shows to take your mind
off entertainment.

*Sign at entrance to a weight-watchers' class in Manchester,
England:*
'Weigh In'

In a sports shop in Brighton:
Don't be mean to your mother-in-law. Buy her a surfboard.

At a garden centre in Auckland, New Zealand:
'Remember, we are your growing concern'

Wartime notice in grocer's shop in the English Midlands:
To prevent hoarding, we have raised the price of sugar.

Sign in window of an optician's:
If you can't see what you what, you're at the right shop.

Above a dog-kennel in San Diego:
Beware of the Mailman!

In a field in Galloway, Scotland:
Trespassers Admitted. Our bull will charge later.

Notice in a fortune-teller's booth on Blackpool's Golden Mile:
Gipsy Zandra will not be here this August – She is going to
have a 'flu virus.

In a cafe in the English Lake District:
High Teas, Upstairs.

In an elevator in New York:
No pushing except in an emergency.

On the side of a milk float in St Helier, Jersey:
From MOO to YOU in an HOUR or TWO.

On the wall of a company director's office:
Staff members who are pulling their weight will never have
any to throw around.

On a notice-board in a church hall in Swansea, Wales:
The speaker for next Sunday evening's service will be nailed on the church door.

Notice in waiting-room of a Beverly Hills doctor:
Don't Just Sit There – Meditate!

In an evening newspaper in Manchester:
Wanted: Good Home for Pedigreed Siamese Cat, male neutered owner going abroad.

In reception room of a London psychiatrist:
Be Yourself! There Isn't Anyone Better Qualified.

Outside a disco in Plymouth:
Fastest Fun in the West.

In an insurance office in Vancouver:
It's Amazing How Much Good A Man Can Do If He Doesn't Care Who Gets the Credit.

On a sign-painter's shop in Paisley, Scotland:
We Made Signs Before We Could Talk.

In a New York restaurant:
Etiquette is knowing which fingers to put in your mouth when you whistle for the waiter.

In fish shop, above filleted kippers:
Delicious . . . No Bones About It.

Poster on a billboard in California:
Please Note – Bill Posters Will Be Prosecuted.

In a government building in London:
Income Tax Office – Sorry, Open.

At a funeral undertaker's:
Join Our Christmas Club.

On a drinking fountain in Nevada:
'Old Faceful'

On a fortune-teller's door:
Medium charges Medium Prices.

On a street with four rival petrol stations:
Last Chance to Fill Up for 50 Metres.

For Sale notice in window:
Used Bicycle for Girl with Leather Seat.

In a pub in Southampton:
Messages from Wives and Loved Ones Taken in Rough Translation. Verbatim cannot be guaranteed.

Notice on a stall at a London street-market:
Large cage, suitable for a bloody big budgie.

Notice in driving-school:
Now you've passed your test, don't try and pass everything.

Sign in dairy in Kilmarnock, Scotland:
If our eggs were any 'fresher,' they'd be insulting.

On rear of a very small red-coloured car:
When I grow up, all I want is to be a fire engine.

In window of a pet shop in Edmonton, Canada:
We are closing down on expiry of leash.

Notice in a Hollywood film-trade weekly:
"Chorus girl 43-22-28 would like to meet man with $432,228."

FORGET IT, BUDDY, YOU'RE FIFTY BUCKS SHORT!

Notice in reception area of an Inland Revenue office:
Be sure you don't misCOUNT your blessings.

On a promotions notice-board in a London office:
The toughest thing about success is that you've got to keep on being a success.

On a managing-director's desk in Birmingham:
My real genius is an infinite capacity for picking YOUR brains.

On a tennis-player's T-shirt:
Cupid, beware! Love Means Nothing to Me.

Notice in a bar:
If angry wives call, our answering-service charges are –
'Just left' – 15p
'He's on his way' – 35p
'He's not here' – £1
'Who did you say?' – £2

On the gate of a private house in North London:
Beware of dog! His bite is worse than his bark.

In plumber's window in Manchester, England:
We won't flush out your bank but we will make your
goodies go round the bend.

Sign on a muddy lane in Cornwall:
Beware, CONGEALED Turning.

On a company director's desk in Toronto:
Remind me never to put off until tomorrow the things I've
already put off until today.

Above a stall at garden fete in Harrogate, Yorkshire:
Try our Cakes and Bum Competition.

In a marriage-guidance office in Melbourne:
Husbands, you are really broken-in when you understand
every word your wife ISN'T saying!

On a washing-machine in a Belfast launderette:
This machine is permanently out of order.

In a dignified hotel near Geneva:
Our Guests Are Kindly Requested to Avoid Making
Rumours in the Room.

IT'S NOT A RUMOUR — IT'S A FACT!

Sign in garden of a luxury home in Surrey:
For Sale, Rolls-Royce car. Used only in front of house by rich couple as status symbol.

Sign in café in Majorca:
Peoples Must Be Inside and Seated to Order Drinks and Dance.

Notice in a delicatessen in New York:
If You Can't Smell What You Want, Go See an Ear, Nose and Throat Man!

Outside a used-car showroom in Glasgow:
Sports Car For Sale. Ask for Hamish, the Guy with the Bad Back.

On a temporary fencing in front of excavations in Chicago:
Spectators Are Requested Not to Fall into Excavation So As Not to Injure Workmen.

In a birth-control clinic:
She who indulges, bulges . . .

In a committee room:
If you have an open mind, don't close it for repair.

Sign carried by an Arsenal supporter at the 1979 FA Cup Final:
Show Us Your Cheek, Arsenal!

In a theatrical agency:
If at first you don't succeed, why not give up . . . !

At a salespersons' convention in Detroit:
Never wait for something to turn up – Get busy and turn it up yourself.

In the window of a shop in Carlisle:
Don't get overcharged in other shops – come in here.

On a notice-board in a city office:
It is not the company's policy to let employees go home Friday nights as tired as they come in on Monday mornings.

In a TV repair shop:
Mend your own telly – then bring it to us.

On a church bulletin board:
If you keep your mouth shut, you won't put your foot in it.

Warning notice on electricity pylon in West Germany:
Anybody touching will be killed instantly.
Scrawled below:
Anybody ignoring this notice will be sent to prison for eight days.

Outside a farm near Bristol:
Dog needed for milking cows.

Notice above the smashed window of a Birmingham store:
Business as usual. Drive right in. Our last customer did!

Sign at a petrol-service station in England's West Country:
Ring twice for NIGHT service. Then keep your shirt on
while I put my pants on!

In a village pub:
If you want to pull the wool over your wife's eyes, be sure to
use a good yarn.

Wayside pulpit notice outside New York:
At the last count, gossip was running down more people
than automobiles.

In a bookshop in Aberdeen:
Buy your Christmas gift books now and have plenty of time
to read them first.

In a church magazine:
The old churchyard has been sadly neglected because there have been no burials for 20 years. Please encourage everyone to remedy the situation.

In a senior citizens' club in Portsmouth:
Old age is like everything else. To make a success of it, you've got to start young.

In a marriage-guidance bureau:
Matrimony was the first union to defy management.

On a company director's desk in Toronto:
Confidence is the feeling you have before you know better.

On a wayside pulpit in New Zealand:
Nobody can walk backwards into the future.

In a London psychiatrist's:
Remember the tortoise – you only make headway if you stick your neck out.

In a New York beautician's:
Why tell your true age? You'll only add years to your life.

Sign in a restaurant in Malta:
We will allow you to pick and chews.

On a medical college notice-board at Edinburgh:
Anatomy section closed due to strike. Skeleton service available.

In a factory at Auckland, New Zealand:
During working hours staff are not allowed to eat anything outside the canteen except the gate-house attendant.

On door of a betting-shop in Motherwell, Scotland:
Back at ten to one.

In a marriage bureau in Melbourne:
Better to have loved a short girl than never to have loved a tall.

In a car-repair yard in Manchester:
You crash 'em . . . We'll bash 'em!

In another car-repair shop:
Your carelessness leads to carlessness . . .

In a café in Toronto:
Customers who wish to put cigarette ash in their cup should first call a waiter . . . He will be delighted to pour your coffee into the ash-tray.

Notice in a department store in Bristol:
Customers who are willing to pay just that little more and are looking for a really fascinating out-of-the-ordinary pet should try the second floor and ask to see our Miss Mortimer.

Notice to be inscribed on the tombstone of Lew Lewis, a comedian from Northampton, England, as instructed in his will:
'Lew Lewis, the comedian, died here for the last time!'

Notice in antique shop at Windermere, England:
We have new items every Monday.

Sign outside petrol station:
Last Garage Until The Next One.

In a marriage bureau in Brisbane, Australia:
Our clients win years and years of married Blitz!

Notice in interior decorator's:
We do everything on the house.

Notice in debt-collector's office in Leeds:
If one half of the world knew how the other half lived, they
wouldn't pay their bills either.

Outside a petrol station near Manchester:
Warning: Politicians can damage your wealth.

In a doctor's surgery in Edmonton, Canada:
For fast-acting relief, why not try slowing down?

For Sale sign in Darlington:
Baker's business. Large oven, present owner has been in it for seven years.

Sign at a fairground trampoline stand:
Senior citizens over 70, no charge!